FOCUS ON
PAKISTAN

Mano Rumalshah

Evans Brothers Limited

Published by Evans Brothers Limited
2A Portman Mansions
Chiltern Street
London W1M 1LE

First published in Great Britain in 1989 by
Hamish Hamilton Children's Books

Reprinted 1992, 1994, 1999

Design by Andrew Shoolbred
Map by Tony Garrett

The author and publishers would like to thank Heidi Larson
for all her help in the preparation of this book

Printed in Hong Kong by Dah Hua Printing Co. Ltd.

ISBN 0 237 60193 1

Acknowledgements
The author and publishers would like to thank the following for
permission to reproduce the photographs: Nick Birch cover;
Camerapix title page, 6 (left), 11 (right), 19 (left), 18, 21 (above),
24 (right); Prodeepta Das 14 (right), 19 (left), 30; Beryl Dhanjal 7,
27 (above); Heidi Larson contents page, 6 (right), 10, 11 (left), 12,
13 (left), 14, 15, 16, 17, 19 (right), 20, 21 (below), 22, 23, 24 (left),
25, 26, 27 (below), 28, 29, 31; Stephen Olsson 9 (below); NHPA 9
(above); Zefa 8.

The author and publisher would like to thank
Heidi Larson for all her help in
the preparation of this book.

Cover Doorway to the Badshahi Mosque, Lahore. One
of Pakistan's most famous buildings, the mosque has a
huge courtyard where 10,000 people can gather to pray.
It dates from the 17th century and the decoration is
typical of the Mughal period.

Title page The Minar-e-Pakistan in Lahore marks the
spot where the first resolution for the creation of Pakistan
was proposed by the All India Muslim League on
23 March 1940. It stands in the Iqbal Park, not far from
the Lahore Fort and the Badshahi Mosque.

Opposite Mountains dominate the scenery of northern
Pakistan. Some of the world's highest peaks are found
here, including K2 which is rated as the second highest
mountain after Everest.

Contents

Introducing Pakistan

Pakistan stretches from the Himalaya and Karokoram mountains to the Arabian Sea. It is the land of the Indus River which saw the rise of some of the earliest civilisations in the world.

Pakistan has been described as the crossroads of Asia. Over the centuries, many travellers from India, China and Europe have passed through these lands in search of new territories.

Birth of a nation

In 1930 a great philosopher-poet called Muhammad Iqbal made a very important suggestion. He had the idea of creating a separate Muslim state in the Indian subcontinent. Seventeen years later, on 14 August 1947, Pakistan ('Land of the Pure') was created as a Muslim homeland, separate from Hindu-dominated India. Pakistan's first leader was *Quaid-i-Azam* (Great Leader) Mohammad Ali Jinnah.

It is unusual to create a country for a particular religious group. Pakistan was also a special case because it consisted of two areas which lay 2000 kilometres apart, called East and West Pakistan. In 1971, East Pakistan became an independent country. This is now Bangladesh.

Today Pakistan has a population of about 121 million people, spread over an area of 803,950 square kilometres. It is a land of great contrasts. You can travel from the high peaks and freezing cold of the north to the deserts and extreme heat of the Punjab and Sind.

Provinces of Pakistan

Pakistan is divided into four provinces, each with its own distinctive people, language and culture. Baluchistan is the largest province but it has the smallest population. It is rich in natural resources.

The North West Frontier Province is perhaps the most romantic of the four provinces. Many stories have been written about the Pushtuns of this area. Their bravery and rugged lifestyle have become legendary. Adjoining North West Frontier Province are the Northern Areas which are administered separately. These include the beautiful valleys of Chitral and Hunza.

Over half the people in Pakistan live in the province of Punjab, which is rich in agriculture and industry. In 1947 the original Punjab was split in two by the new Pakistan-Indian border.

The province of Sind has been inhabited for thousands of years. Much of Sind is desert, but there are substantial farming areas along the Indus. With its historic past, Sind is rich in culture and tradition.

Many different languages are spoken in Pakistan, but Urdu is the official language. English is also widely spoken in commerce and government.

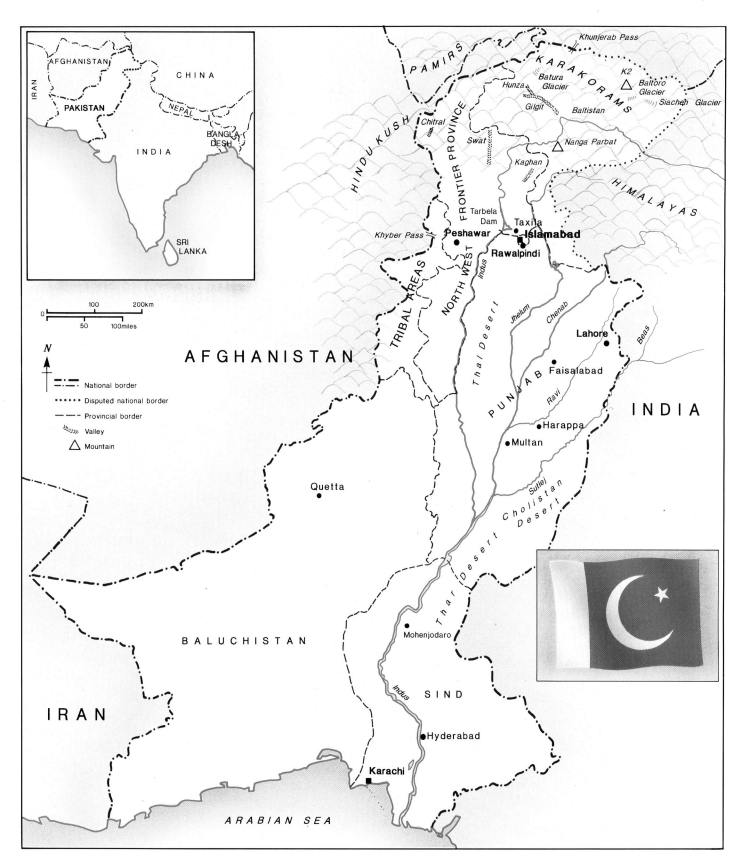

AFGHANISTAN
IRAN
CHINA
NEPAL
INDIA
BANGLA DESH
PAKISTAN
SRI LANKA

100   200km
0
50   100miles

N

National border
Disputed national border
Provincial border
Valley
Mountain

PAMIRS
KARAKORAMS
Khunjerab Pass
K2
Baltoro Glacier
Batura Glacier
Hunza
Siacheh Glacier
Gilgit
Baltistan
HINDU KUSH
Chitral
Swat
Nanga Parbat
FRONTIER PROVINCE
Kaghan
HIMALAYAS
Tarbela Dam
Taxila
Khyber Pass
Peshawar
Islamabad
Rawalpindi
TRIBAL AREAS
NORTH WEST
Indus
Jhelum
Chenab
Lahore
Beas
Thal Desert
PUNJAB
Faisalabad
Ravi
INDIA
AFGHANISTAN
Harappa
Multan
Quetta
Sutlej
Cholistan Desert
Thar Desert
BALUCHISTAN
Mohenjodaro
SIND
IRAN
Indus
Hyderabad
Karachi
ARABIAN SEA

5

Pakistan is one of the most richly historical areas in the world. The Indus Valley was the site of one of the oldest and most advanced of ancient civilisations. Since then, the country has been invaded countless times. Over the centuries, different people have brought their own languages, customs and religions. These have all contributed to the cultural heritage of modern Pakistan.

The Indus people

The Indus Valley was the cradle of South Asian civilisation. We now know that a very sophisticated group of people lived here between 3000 and 2000 BC. At the turn of the century the ancient sites at Mohenjodaro and Harappa were excavated for the first time. Archaeologists found large granaries, a college for priests and other buildings which may have been

A seal from Harappa. The ancient script of the Indus Valley has still not been deciphered.

palaces and citadels. They were built with baked bricks and served by an elaborate drainage system. The Indus people lived in a highly organised society based on farming and trade. Their artistic skills can be seen in the fine pottery and sculpture on display in museums. This civilisation flourished until the Aryans invaded from the north.

Taxila

One of the many influential invasions of the region was led by Alexander the Great, the famous Greek leader. He arrived in 327 BC, but Greek rule did not last long. Later Ashoka, the great Buddhist king, took control of the region. Taxila was then an important cultural centre. It is now a

famous archaeological site with a fine museum. Here you can see the remains of Buddhist monasteries and stupas. The museum contains some priceless works of art from the period, as well as tools, kitchen utensils and toys. This period is known as the Gandhara Civilisation.

Muslims and Mughals

In AD 711 a Muslim Arab general called Muhammad bin Qasim landed on the coast near Karachi. He was the first person to lead an invasion from the sea. From the 10th century onwards numerous other Muslims came from Central Asia. Gradually these people sowed the seeds of their culture and religion. They began to take control of the local population and started to run the country.

The Mughals were Muslims who came from Asia Minor. In the 16th century they established an empire which is now regarded as one of the Golden Ages of the Indian subcontinent. Many beautiful mosques, forts, palaces and gardens were built by the Mughals and some still survive today. During this period people were generally prosperous and arts and culture flourished. The Mughal Empire started to fade in the 18th century. By the mid-19th century all of present-day Pakistan was under British rule and remained so until 1947.

Right: The Lahore Fort was built by Emperor Akbar in 1566. The huge walls enclose a series of lawns and courtyards, built by later Mughal Emperors. These include the Diwan-i-Khas (Hall of Private Audience), the Diwan-i-Aam (Hall of Public Audience) and the Shish Mahal (Hall of Mirrors). The most beautiful parts of the fort were built by Emperor Shah Jehan, who also built the Taj Mahal in India.

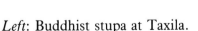
Left: Buddhist stupa at Taxila.

Mountains, valleys and passes

Pakistan has some of the finest mountain ranges in the world. They are found in the north, where four great ranges meet. These are the Himalayas, the Karakorams, the Pamirs and the Hindu Kush. They radiate out like the spokes of a wheel.

High peaks

The most famous mountain range is the Himalayas, said to form the 'roof of the world'. They extend from Pakistan, eastwards across India and Nepal. Nanga Parbat is the highest Himalayan peak in Pakistan.

The Karakoram Range is said to have the greatest concentration of lofty mountains in the world. The highest peak of this range is K2 (8611m), which is thought to be the second highest mountain in the world, after Everest.

There is a famous site at the head of the Baltoro Glacier where four peaks form a kind of basin, or 'amphitheatre'.

Glaciers

Pakistan has some of the largest glaciers outside the Arctic. The three most famous are the Siachen, the Batura and the Baltoro. These enormous glaciers form ice corridors. One section of Baltoro is called 'Cathedrals of Baltoro' because its sharp ridges look like spires.

Valleys

Not surprisingly, the region has some beautiful natural valleys. The most famous are Swat, Kaghan, Baltistan, Gilgit, Hunza and Chitral. These attractive areas are increasingly becoming a 'playground' for people from the West. Polo is one of the most popular team games, but tourists spend most of their time mountaineering, trekking and hiking. Fishing is also becoming a popular sport.

Snow leopard in the mountains.

The local population are rugged mountain people with a distinctive culture. They are generally healthy and many live to a great age. Some of the most fascinating people in these valleys are the Kafir-Kalash in Chitral Valley. They are said to be descended from a very ancient non-Muslim tribe. Historians have had great arguments about their origins. According to legend, they are descended from the soldiers of Alexander the Great. People have found similarities between their traditions and local legends and those of Ancient Greece.

Passes

For centuries the mountain passes of the North West Frontier were the gateway to the Indian subcontinent. Invaders such as Alexander the Great and the Mughals used these passes. The most famous of all is the Khyber Pass which lies a few kilometres from Peshawar and opens the way to Afghanistan. Another famous pass is the Khunjerab Pass which opens the way to the ancient 'silk route' between China and Pakistan. Some of the great explorers of the past have used this route, including Marco Polo the Venetian trader.

Above: Mother and child in Chitral Valley.

Left: Lush terraces in Hunza Valley.

Plains and rivers

Beneath the lofty peaks and passes, down towards the south, spread the vast plains of the Indus River Basin. This area includes the provinces of the North West Frontier, Punjab and Sind.

The Indus

The River Indus runs for almost 2720 km from its source in the mountains to its delta on the Arabian Sea. Over the centuries this river has seen the rise and fall of many civilisations and today it remains the life-line of this ancient, fertile region. This area produces the country's main food and cash crops. It is also the site of the country's main industrial complexes.

The River Indus is vital to the economy of modern Pakistan, just as it was to the people who lived here about 4000 years ago.

Right: The Tarbela Dam is the largest earth-filled dam in the world. It has created a reservoir more than 80 km long that provides drinking water and hydro-electric power.

Below: A cotton plant in the Punjab.

Land of Five Waters

The heartland of the region is the Punjab (meaning 'land of five waters'). This is the agricultural and industrial centre of the country. It has a population of about 68 million. The 'five waters' are the Rivers Jhelum, Chenab, Ravi, Sutlej and Beas. These rivers are interlinked with a network formed by one of the finest irrigation systems of the world. The system is based on a series of barrages and dams. In 1977 construction was completed on the Tarbela Dam on the River Indus. These dams provide hydro-electric power as well as water.

The Plain of Punjab is very fertile and accessible. In spite of all its fertility, it has two small deserts called Cholistan and Thal and can be very hot and dusty. The deserts are now being cultivated and made to bloom.

The Punjab also has some of the largest cities in the country: Lahore, Rawalpindi and Faisalabad. Multan, towards the south is the gateway to Sind.

Sind

About 19 million people live on the vast Plain of Sind. Most of the land is sandy and there is a large desert called Thar. Most people live around the River Indus which forms its delta in the southernmost part of the province. In recent years land reclamation and new irrigation schemes have helped the area to make the most of its agricultural potential.

Farming and food

Pakistan is still a rural country, in spite of the recent growth of industry. Around 72% of the population still live in rural areas and 51% earn their living through agriculture. Women play an active part in agricultural activities and some tasks, such as cotton-picking, are reserved exclusively for them.

Crops

Over the last 10 years, farming has become more and more productive. The country has become self-sufficient in essential foods and it now also exports food to other countries. Pakistan is one of the world's major rice exporters and produces one of its finest varieties, Basmati rice. Other important agricultural exports include cotton and fish, especially prawns.

The country is still not self-sufficient in meat and dairy products, but farmers are now developing this side of their business.

North and south

The main region for farming is the Indus Basin, a large area of flat land spread over the provinces of Punjab and Sind. An artificial system of canals and dams has helped to make the land more fertile and productive.

Wheat, maize, corn and rice are harvested in the summer months, while cotton and sugar cane are harvested during the winter. Cereals, lentils and oil seeds are

An array of fresh fruit and vegetables in Peshawar.

also produced. In recent years farmers have started to grow more fruits, including mangoes, bananas and apples. Most popular of all are citrus fruits, such as oranges and lemons. In high seasons you can see fruit 'mountains' on the roadside.

Baluchistan and North West Frontier are best known for producing nuts and dried fruits. Peaches, pears and pomegranates are also grown in these areas.

Modernisation

Until very recently, traditional farming methods were used throughout Pakistan. You still see working animals such as oxen, buffaloes, cows and donkeys everywhere you go. This is now changing rapidly as more agricultural machinery is being introduced and more fertilisers are used.

The Government of Pakistan is trying to encourage modernisation and raise the standard of living in rural areas. There are programmes to improve health care, water supply, sanitation, roads and electrification.

Favourite foods

The daily diet of 98% of the population consists of bread, meat, rice, vegetables and lentils. There are several varieties of bread. The most common are 'naan' and 'chapati'.

Different regions have their own specialities. Food in the Plains is usually highly spiced. In the northern areas grilled meats and milder foods are popular. There are different sorts of curries and kebabs. Most Pakistanis are Muslims, so they only eat Halal meat, which has been specially slaughtered. Muslims do not eat pork or drink alcohol. In the Punjab many villagers still cook with traditional clay ovens called 'tandoors'. People all over the world now recognise the word 'tandoori' as a hallmark of Pakistani and Indian cookery.

Making samosas in a city home.

Carrot Halva
A delicious carrot dessert

Ingredients
Carrots 900g (2 lb)
Full cream milk 2.2 litres (4 pints)
Cinnamon 1 cm (½ inch) stick
Butter 50g (2 oz)
Sugar 225g (8 oz)
Blanched almonds 50g (2 oz)
Cardamom seeds 3
Raisins 50g (2 oz)

Method
Grate the carrots. Heat the milk, carrots and cinnamon together and boil for one minute. Turn down the heat and simmer, stirring frequently with a wooden spoon. When the milk is reduced to less than a quarter, stir in the cardamoms and raisins. Mix and stir until the mixture is quite dry. Add the butter, stirring all the time and then the sugar. Stir and cook for about 10 minutes until the mixture is a rich red colour. Add the almonds and serve hot or cold.

Making chapatis in a village home.

Industry and energy

When Pakistan was created in 1947 it had hardly any industry at all. Since then it has made enormous progress. Today, the country has built up a vast industrial base, second only to agriculture in terms of national economy.

Industry

Pakistan is now self-sufficient in several essential consumer goods. It is also making rapid progress in heavy industry. Textile production is now particularly important, followed by fertilisers, leather products, carpets and cement. The country has also invested in chemical plants and oil refineries. There are well-equipped assembly plants for foreign-made trucks, tractors and cars. For many years Pakistan has been manufacturing railway carriages and rolling stock. The new steel plant at

In Pakistan furniture design varies from region to region.

Leather goods are an important export product.

Port Qasim near Karachi will give a further boost to metal-based industries.

On a smaller scale Pakistan is also successful in the manufacture of high-quality sports goods and surgical instruments. Traditional cottage industries, based on centuries of craftsmanship, are also important. Every effort is being made to keep these industries viable. The most important crafts are furniture-making, pottery, metalwork, embroidery, carpet weaving and wood carving.

Energy

Although Pakistan has made rapid advances in technology since 1947, it still lacks the main resource to service its industries. Pakistan has an acute energy shortage. In spite of many new schemes the country still experiences continual power shut-downs and is unable to bridge the gap between supply and demand. Pakistan has very limited amounts of 'fossil' fuels, such as oil and coal. The cost of importing oil from abroad accounts for 50% of the country's import budget. The country's natural gas is needed for the production of fertilisers and in the petrochemical industry. There is little to spare for power generating. At the moment hydro-electric power is the main source of energy, but it cannot meet the country's growing needs.

In the face of this problem, the Pakistani authorities have started to develop nuclear energy. This is a controversial choice, but they feel that there is no alternative. While nuclear power may help to solve Pakistan's energy shortage, many people are concerned about the effect it will have on the environment.

A display of fine traditional copperware.

Transport

A visitor to Pakistan would immediately be struck by the variety of its transport systems. These range from carts and rickshaws to luxurious air-conditioned cars and modern aeroplanes. And the most intriguing thing is the way they all exist side by side, each one with its own function.

By air

Pakistan is well established on the international travel map. International airlines use it as a major stopover place in the East. Pakistan has an efficient airline of its own, called Pakistan International Airlines (PIA). It covers different parts of the world and also offers a substantial air network within the country. It can take you to all the cities and even to some of the major towns. It also offers the vital air service to the remote northern areas of the country, which are usually inaccessible to any other forms of transport. Air travel has come of age in Pakistan and people use it extensively for business and leisure purposes.

By rail

Railways are important in Pakistan. The present system has been modernised and extended from the original system which was developed during the British raj. Now almost all the towns and cities can be reached by rail and the network totals about 8,775 kilometres.

A train journey across Pakistan is still quite an exciting experience. The big crowds at the railway stations and the cry of the 'hawkers' like the 'chai-wala' (tea vendor) create a special atmosphere.

By road

Nowadays public buses are also important in Pakistan. Apart from the remote mountain areas, most of the country is accessible by bus. Lorries are also important for transporting goods. The road system covers a total length of 104,323 kilometres, but it still needs to be extended.

Private cars and buses are increasingly important in the cities. Car ownership has

In cities, rickshaws are particularly popular.

increased in recent years, but it is still the privilege of the affluent. Japanese cars dominate this market. An ordinary bicycle is still the most widely used vehicle all over the country.

Rickshaws and tongas

A more traditional way of getting about is provided by rickshaws and tongas. A rickshaw is usually a converted scooter with seating for two people. It serves very well as a cheap taxi service. The oldest and most romantic vehicle is the tonga, a horse-driven cart. If the horse is properly cared for and the cart properly maintained, this can be a pleasant way of getting about.

In big cities carts driven by camels and donkeys are also common. They are

In villages, traditional carts are a familiar sight.

particularly useful for transporting heavy loads in old, narrow streets. In villages the bullock-cart is a timeless symbol of farming life. They move at their own pace and in their own way and are still indispensable in rural communities.

In towns, tongas and bicycles are commonly used.

Culture and customs

Pakistan is a country of great cultural diversity. Over the centuries invaders and settlers from far and wide have brought their own customs and traditions with them. These have all contributed to the cultural life of the country. Arts of all kinds flourish in Pakistan and most of them are influenced by the Islamic religion.

Architecture

There are many beautiful buildings in Pakistan. The Mughals were great patrons

Calligraphy

The art of handwriting, called calligraphy, plays an important part in Islamic culture. Mosques are often decorated with beautifully designed extracts from the Qur'an. The Wazir Khan Mosque in Lahore, shown below, was built in 1634. The floral patterns and verses are made of glazed tiles and enammelled mosaic. The central panel contains the words 'Allah' and 'Muhammad'.

An imposing modern house in Karachi.

of architecture and some of the most famous buildings date from that period. Mughal architecture is renowned for its delicate and intricate designs. Even today, many modern buildings, especially mosques, are influenced by the Mughal style. Commercial buildings, on the other hand, are usually influenced by modern western architecture.

Music and dance

One of the great cultural traditions of Pakistan is Qawali singing. Traditionally performed by groups of men, Qawali used to be important as a means of expressing religious devotion.

There are several types of regional dancing which are still performed today. Khattak dance from the frontier area is still very popular. This dance is often performed with swords. The Bhangra dance from the Punjab is an ancient harvest folk dance which still survives today. Folk dances are performed by women at segregated gatherings.

Festivals

There are three very important times in the Muslim year which are key dates for people in Pakistan. Ramadan is a particularly special time. For a whole month people neither eat nor drink between sunrise and sunset. At the end of Ramadan there is a festival called Eid-ul-Fitr. Children enjoy this festival because they are given presents and sweets. There is also another festival called Eid-ul-Adha, when people sacrifice a goat and share it among family, friends and the needy.

Films

The film industry is still important in Pakistan although videos are now replacing the cinema. Pakistani film-makers usually base their films on stories of romance or adventure. These are particularly popular. Film and TV stars become great celebrities and attract a good deal of attention.

The famous Pakistani film star Shabnum.

Sport and leisure

Pakistan has acquired quite a reputation in the world of sport. Soccer, tennis, badminton, basketball, athletics and wrestling are all popular, but it is in cricket, field-hockey and squash that Pakistan has made its mark.

Cricket

It is cricket which really rouses passions in Pakistan. The whole nation often sits glued to the cricket, especially when Pakistan plays against India. Pakistan is now well respected on the international cricket scene. Over the last decade or so, their cricket has improved dramatically. They have performed successfully against all the cricketing nations. In 1992 Pakistan won the World Cup beating England in the final.

In every back-street and courtyard there is a cricket field. These 'cricket nurseries' have produced a wealth of good natural players, from Hanif Mohammad to Javed Miandad.

Hockey

It was at the Rome Olympics in 1960 that Pakistan first won the gold medal for field hockey. Ever since they have dominated the hockey world, winning more Olympic and World Championships than any other team. The most famous Pakistani player was Colonel Dara, who is regarded as an all-time great.

Squash

Strangely enough, the sport in which Pakistan has really dominated the international scene is scarcely known at home. For the last thirty years or so, Pakistani squash players have ruled the world. The key name in this sport is

Left: Street cricket is a popular pastime for children all over Pakistan.

Right: A range of kites in a colourful shop display.

Khan. The most legendary of them all was Hashim Khan, who started life as a ball boy and went on to win the British Open seven times. He played well into his forties and his astronomical success encouraged other members of his family to follow suit.

Traditional pastimes

Some of the most traditional pastimes include kite-flying, falconry, polo and wrestling. In the winter months kite-flying is very popular; at certain festivals the sky is ablaze with colourful kites. Polo is said to have been invented in these parts, but it got its boost under the British raj. It is especially popular with landed gentry and army officers. Falconry is another sport that appeals to the wealthy and it attracts many rich sheiks from the Gulf States. But wrestling is still the most popular sport among ordinary working people in rural areas.

Jehangir Khan, one of the world's top squash players.

21

Religion

The official religion of Pakistan is Islam and its followers are called Muslims. The country was created in order to provide a homeland for the Muslims of the Indian subcontinent and the great majority of the people (97%) belong to this faith. The main minorities are Ahmadis, Hindus and Christians. The Ahmadis established an Islamic sect in the late 19th century. In 1974 they were declared non-Muslim by official Islam.

The Muslims

The prophet of Islam, Muhammad, was born about AD 570 in the city of Mecca. The first Muslims lived in Arabian countries. It was the Arab general Muhammad bin Qasim who first brought Islam to Sind and the Punjab. During the rule of the Mughals Islam began to spread throughout the area. Its influence, especially through architecture and customs, ran deep into all levels of society.

Muslims belong to two main groups, or denominations: the Sunnis and the Shias. In Pakistan, almost 80% of Muslims are Sunnis. The Shias form a significant minority. (Iran is the largest Shiite country.) There is also a small but influential group called the Ismailis, who follow Agha Khan as their spiritual leader.

Muslim women may go to mosques, but often they pray privately at home.

Muslim customs

All Muslims are expected to live by their religious code, most of which is found in the Qur'an. Islamic religious law is called the Sharia. Traditionally, this law regulates things like marriage, divorce and inheritance. In Pakistan there is a dual system of justice. Both civil courts and religious courts have authority but the Supreme Court is a civil court.

Islam is very much a way of life for most people in Pakistan. There is a Call to Prayer five times a day, when people stop what they are doing to pray. Whenever a plane journey starts, the crew invoke the name of God and say a prayer for a safe journey. During the holy month of Ramadan most people fast.

Islam has strict codes of behaviour for men and women. Women dress modestly and may wear a veil. The position of women in society is a matter of great debate in Pakistan. Islam offers them protection and a privileged status. In certain legal matters, however, a woman's word is considered inferior to a man's. In Pakistan many women work and make an important contribution to the economy.

Other faiths

The Christian Church was introduced in the 19th century by European missionaries. There is, however, some evidence that there were Christians here as early as the

The Badshahi Mosque, Lahore.

1st century AD. Christians work in the professions, like teaching, or do manual jobs. They live mainly in the Punjab.

The Hindus are found mainly in the province of Sind. They are part of the ancient people of the region who, at the time of partition, did not opt for India. They are mainly involved in agriculture and business.

Men worshipping in a mosque.

The Muslim Creed

The basic creed of Islam is belief in one God (Allah, in Arabic). Muhammad is his Prophet. Islam preaches the equality of all human beings. The Islamic holy book is the Qur'an (or Koran). This is written in Arabic and is almost the same size as the Christian New Testament.

The Islamic code is guided by what are called the Five Pillars of Islam. They are:

To believe in Allah and his Prophet Muhammad
To pray five times a day
To fast during the holy month of Ramadan
To give for charitable purposes
To perform pilgrimage (Haj)

Islamabad

Islamabad, the 'abode of Islam', is the capital city of the Islamic Republic of Pakistan. It is one of the newest capital cities in the world and also claims to be the most attractive, although much of it is still in the process of being built.

Setting

The original capital of Pakistan was Karachi, but it was never thought that it would remain the permanent seat of government. The present capital was built near to the much older city of Rawalpindi, just a few kilometres away. These cities lie against the backdrop of the Marghalla hills, in the foothills of the mountains. The area provides a pleasant scenic background, made even more attractive by Rawal Dam. This is a pleasant picnic area, and it also irrigates about 4,000 hectares of surrounding areas and supplies fresh water to Islamabad itself.

Modern young life in the capital.

Sparkling white buildings in Islamabad.

Design

The construction of this new capital began in 1961. Some of the world's most distinguished planners and architects have contributed to its development. The city is well laid out with large public buildings, attractive parks, and wide boulevards lined with trees. It is now firmly established as the capital city of the nation and functions as such. There are about a quarter of a

Inside a mosque

The Muslim place of worship is called a mosque. A mosque usually has a dome and a slender tower called a minaret.

Muslims take off their shoes before they go into the mosque, as a mark of respect to God. They also perform a ritual wash before praying.

Inside the main hall of the mosque is an open space. Prayers are always said facing Mecca, the holy Muslim city. The Imam leads the prayers in the mosque, which are said in Arabic. Men and women worship separately.

The Faisal Mosque was designed to look like a desert tent.

million people living in Islamabad, but it is an expanding city.

Many of the buildings are beautiful, and some are just outstanding. In this category the stunning Faisal Mosque has no rivals. It was designed by a Turkish architect and named after the late King Faisal of Saudi Arabia. It covers an area of 189,705 square metres with 88 metre high minarets and a 40 metre high prayer chamber. The Islamic university has its premises below the courtyard. The whole complex dominates the landscape. There are also several beauty spots in the same area which people use for picnics and outings. The city's rose garden has over 250 different varieties of rose.

Cities

Pakistan is mainly a rural country, but in recent years there has been rapid urban growth. Some of its cities have expanded too quickly while others have developed more steadily.

Karachi

Although no longer the capital of Pakistan, Karachi is still the country's commercial centre. The city has grown considerably and is now an international metropolis, with a population of about 7 million people. It is a busy stopover point for international air traffic. The only coastal city in Pakistan, it has a fine natural harbour. Karachi is the regional capital of Sind. One of its most important sites is the tomb of the Father of the Nation, *Qaid-i-Azam* (Great Leader) Mohammad Ali Jinnah.

Karachi, Pakistan's 'sea city'.

Lahore

The regional capital of the Punjab is often described as the cultural centre of Pakistan. It has many beautiful old buildings, including the Badshahi Mosque, which dates from the 17th century. The Shalimar Gardens are also famous. The Mughals built them in Persian style with pools, fountains and pavilions. There are other sites from the Mughal period, including a fort and a magnificent tomb.

Peshawar

The capital city of the North West Frontier province is also the cultural centre for the Pushtuns (or Pathans) who live in the mountains of the Hindu Kush. Situated only a few kilometres from the Khyber Pass, this city lay in the path of numerous invaders over the centuries. It has been the focus of world attention, as events in neighbouring Afghanistan brought thousands of refugees to the area.

The Pushtuns

The Pushtuns are one of the largest tribal groups in the world, numbering about 15 million in all. They are proud and independent by nature. The Pushtuns follow a strict code of conduct called 'Pushtunwali'. One rule is that they must always be hospitable to any visitors. Another is that they should take revenge if someone harms or insults a member of the family.

The Shalimar Gardens in Lahore,
'city of the plains'.

Quetta

The capital city of Baluchistan lies at an altitude of 1677 metres. In the summer months many people like to retreat to this quiet shady city where the temperature is pleasantly cool. In the winter it is snowy and cold. In 1935 Quetta was almost completely destroyed by an earthquake, so the present town was rebuilt.

Hyderabad

This is the second largest city in Sind and used to be the capital. It is here that you will get a real sense of the Sindhi people and their culture. Hyderabad is a centre for cottage industries and in the bazaar you can buy gold and silver jewellery, Sindhi embroidery and glass bangles, for which the city is particularly well known.

Faisalabad

Formerly called Lyallpur, this city was renamed after the late King Faisal of Saudi Arabia. Faisalabad is the third largest city in the country and is now heavily industrialised. It has become the capital of the textile industry and is sometimes called the 'Manchester of Pakistan'.

Busy street in Peshawar, the 'frontier city'.

27

Education

In Pakistan, education is treasured by the people and by the authorities. It is seen as a ladder which leads to knowledge and to a better standard of living. The authorities are keen for everyone to be educated so that illiteracy becomes a thing of the past.

A growing sector

The basic education system was set up during the British raj, but in recent years it has been adapted to suit the country's present needs. Wherever ppossible, education is compulsory and free. At the latest count, the country has 107,210 primary schools. There are also 8000 mosque schools, for primary education.

There are 6290 middle schools and 4809 high schools. For further and higher education, there are 293 colleges where trades and crafts are taught. There are 22 universities and 470 undergraduate colleges for arts and sciences. There are also about 100 professional institutes where doctors, engineers and lawyers are trained.

Programme for reform

The literacy rate in Pakistan is about 35%. About 47% of the urban population can read, compared with 17% in rural areas. In a Five Point Programme for 1986-1990, the highest priority was given to rural education. This involved opening new schools,

Left: Old university buildings at Peshawar dating from the British raj.

Right: A girls' school in Azad-Kashn.

upgrading existing schools and training staff. Perhaps the most exciting aspect of the programme has been the opening of 22,000 'Nai Roshni' schools. 'Nai Roshni' means New Light and these schools are designed to give a second chance to people who previously dropped out of school.

In spite of all these efforts, many people choose to pay for private education in Pakistan and it has become big business. In cities there are hundreds of privately operated schools which cater to high school levels. Ordinary people are becoming more and more anxious to send their children to private schools where lessons are usually given in English. They believe that fluency in English will open up many opportunities they would not otherwise have.

A classroom scene.

Going to school

In Pakistan children start school in Class One when they are five years old. They go on to Class Ten when they take their Matriculation Exam. In almost all schools lessons are given in Urdu, which is the national language. For quite a number of children this is not their first language. This can also make it difficult for children to compete at degree level, where all teaching is still in English.

Boys and girls often study together in primary schools, but after that single-sex education is encouraged.

Pakistan and the world

Pakistan is a proud country, rich in culture and tradition. Throughout its history, many different civilisations have intermingled on its soil. Today it is eager to share something of its heritage with the rest of the world.

An Islamic nation

Pakistan is particularly keen to play a leading role in the affairs of the Islamic world. It has become pre-eminent as a Muslim country and continues to promote global Islamic ideals. It plays an important role in the religious and social issues which face Muslim people everywhere. Pakistan is also one of the leading Islamic countries in terms of military power.

For the past couple of decades Pakistan has also played an important role in the Arab oil economy. Many people from Pakistan are now working in the Gulf region and their earnings also contribute greatly to Pakistan's economy.

Government

Pakistan gained independence in 1947 and in 1956 the Islamic Republic of Pakistan was declared. The country has a president and a prime minister, with a parliamentary system. There are four provinces, each with its own governor and chief minister. The provinces are sub-divided into smaller districts for administrative purposes. At

The Habib Bank Plaza in Karachi.

times the army has taken over the running of the country. In 1988 parliamentary democracy was restored when Benazir Bhutto became prime minister, the first Muslim woman leader of modern times.

Pakistan welcomed Afghan refugees for ten years during the 1980s.

India and Afghanistan

Pakistan's relations with two of its neighbours are very important. It shares a long border with India and these two countries are also tied by thousands of years of history. When India and Pakistan were divided in 1947 some thorny issues remained unresolved. The two countries have always fought over Kashmir, which both claim as theirs. If problems like this could be resolved, the two countries could develop a harmonious relationship which would greatly benefit the region.

In the 1980s people around the world watched events in neighbouring Afghanistan very closely. During the Russian occupation of Afghanistan almost 3 million refugees came across the border into Pakistan. Some of these refugees are gradually returning.

Pakistanis abroad

Many people from Pakistan have made their homes in different parts of the world, such as Canada and the United States. There are now about half-a-million Pakistanis in Britain, living mainly in London and the northern cities of Bradford and Manchester. Their distinct Islamic way of life has made its impression on modern Britain. In recent years many beautiful new mosques have been constructed, adding a new dimension to the British landscape.

Index and summary

Population:	120.84 million (72% rural; 28% urban)
Area:	803,950 square km
Bordering:	Iran, Afghanistan, China and India
Capital:	Islamabad
Main cities:	Karachi, Lahore, Islamabad/Rawalpindi, Peshawar, Quetta
Provinces:	Sind (pop. 19 mil.; 141,000 sq.km.); Punjab (pop. 48 mil.; 206,000 sq.km.); North West Frontier (pop. 10.8 mil.; 74,500 sq.km.); Baluchistan (pop. 5.3 mil.; 347,000 sq.km.;
Northern areas:	Baltistan, Gilgit, Hunza and Chitral Valley (pop. 527,000; 28,000 sq.km); Azad ("Free") Jammu and Kashmir (pop. 1.9 mil.; 11,639 sq.km.)
State religion:	Islam (Minorities: Hindus, Sikhs, Christians, Pharsees, Kailash "Kafirs")
State language:	Urdu
Main regional languages:	Punjabi (60%), Sindhi (13%); Pashtu (8%), Baluchi, Brahvi and Dradic Languages in Baluchistan and Northern Areas
Main river:	Indus, 2720 km
Five major tributaries:	Jhelum, Chenab, Ravi, Beas and Sutlej.